THE
ENIGMATICAL
SPHERE
OF
EL CHUPA-KU
EL ESFERA ENIGMATICA DE
EL CHUPA-KU

THE
ENIGMATICAL SPHERE
OF
EL CHUPA-KU
EL ESFERA ENIGMATICA DE EL CHUPA-KU

[one century of chupacabra haiku]

[un siglo de haiku chupacabras]

Juan Manuel Pérez

El Chupacabras Poet Laureate

El Poeta Laureado De Chupacabras

ISBN: 978-1-968958-01-5
First Edition | 2025

Cover art by Louie Perez III

Space Cowboy Books
61871 29 Palms Hwy.
Joshua Tree, CA 92252
www.spacecowboybooks.com

Haiku in this collection have appeared in the following:

Los haiku de esta colección han aparecido en lo siguiente:

Aphelion: The Webzine Of Science Fiction And Fantasy

Boundless: The Anthology Of The Rio Grande Valley International Poetry Festival

El Chupacabra Times

Friday Night Haiku Theater Facebook Project

Snakeskin Poetry Webzine

Speculations III: Poetry From The Weird Poetry Society

Star*Line: The Journal Of The Science Fiction & Fantasy Poetry Association

Terror House Magazine

Unleash Your Inner Chupacabra: A Poetry Anthology By The Members Of The San Angelo Writers' Club

Writers Of The Rio Grande.com

there, for after all
much more than one way to skin
el chupacabras

ahí, porque después de todo
mucho más qué una forma de despellejar
el chupacabras

extinction dismissed
gray, *chupacabra*-skin boots
I want a pair too

extinción desestimada
botas grises de piel de chupacabras
yo también quiero un par

the almighty wrath
standing great, grand *Chupa-Khan*
defecating on your lawn

la ira todopoderosa
de pie el gran Chupa-Khan
defecando en tu césped

Billy goats beware
a second full moon of Fall
Chupacabra Moon

cabritos, cuidado
una segunda luna llena de otoño
Luna de Chupacabras

el chupacabras
sees his shadow and predicts
an apocalypse

el chupacabras
ve su sombra y predice
un apocalipsis

abracadabra
el chupacabras wants to
reach out and grab ya'

abracadabra
el chupacabras quiere
acercarse y agarrarte

chupacabras writes:
"It's Not Easy Being Gray"
as the whole world scoffs

chupacabras escribe:
"No es fácil ser gris"
mientras el mundo entero se burla

sacrificial goat
for a *Chupacabra Cult*
dying for your sins

cabra de sacrificio
por un culto de chupacabras
muriendo por tus pecados

no creative mind
no cryptozoology
no *chupacabras*

sin mente creativa
sin criptozoología
sin chupacabras

on cold winter nights
within the dead mesquite woods
chupacabra growls

en las frías noches de invierno
dentro del bosque de mezquites muertos
gruñe el chupacabras

Godzilla wakes up
a *Giant Chupacabra*
topsy-turvy world

Godzilla despierta
un chupacabras gigante
un mundo al revés

old King Kong versus
the *Giant Chupacabra*
comparing B.O.

el viejo King Kong contra
el chupacabras gigante
comparando el olor corporal

radioactive
chupacabra bites human
Chupa-Man is born

radioactivo
chupacabras muerde a un humano
nace el Hombre-Chupa

Chupacabra Flats:
a new Tex-Mex colony
on red planet Mars

Llano de Chupacabras:
una nueva colonia Tex-Mex
en Marte, el planeta rojo

chupacabra crawl:
obnoxious name for a dance
drunk on tequila

rastreo del chupacabras:
nombre desagradable para un baile
borracho con tequila

chupacabra sits
by the big, old mesquite tree
so laugh; it's your song

chupacabras se sienta
junto al gran árbol de mezquite
ríete; es tu canción

the fight of the year
El Chupacabras versus
Maryland's Goat Man

la pelea del año
El Chupacabras contra
El Hombre Cabra de Maryland

red liquid courage
one too many Billy goats
drunk *chupacabra*

valor de líquido rojo
demasiados cabritos
chupacabras borracho

October the Fifth
is "Take Your *Chupacabra*
To School Or Work Day!"

5 de octubre
¡Lleva tu chupacabras
a la escuela o al trabajo!

personal ad reads:
must enjoy *chupacabra*
goat farm optional

el anuncio personal dice:
hay que disfrutar del chupacabras
granja de cabras opcional

personal ad reads:
single *chupacabras* seeks
fatalistic goat

el anuncio personal dice:
chupacabras soltero busca
cabra fatalista

personal ad reads:
young *chupacabras* seeking
like-minded sucker

el anuncio personal dice:
joven chupacabras buscando
chupador de ideas afines

strangers in the night
chupacabras, goat, farmer
someone's going down

extraños en la noche
chupacabras, cabra, granjero
alguien va a caer

el chupacabras
like childish nature alive
mystery always

el chupacabras
como la naturaleza infantil y viva
siempre un misterio

the goats are always
fatter on the other side
of the farmer's fence

las cabras siempre estan
mas gordas en el otro lado
de la cerca del granjero

"Go tell it on the
Great Chupacabra Mountain"
an accepting goat

"Ve a contarlo a la
Gran Montaña de el Chupacabras"
cabra aceptadora

"We Only Serve Goats!"
sign at the prejudiced hotel
Chupacabras Inn

"¡Solo servimos cabras!"
póster en el hotel prejuicioso
Posada de el Chupacabras

"Chickens Are Welcomed!"
new head chef at *Conchitas*
el chupacabras

🐐

"¡Las gallinas son bienvenidas!"
nuevo jefe de cocina en Conchitas
el chupacabras

el chupacabras:
bastard child of Cthulhu
and Olmec *nagual*

el chupacabras:
hijo bastardo de cthulhu
y nagual olmeca

el chupacabras:
Scary Monsters' Magazine's
Monster Of The Year

el chupacabras:
Revista de Scary Monsters
monstruo del año

el chupacabras
the ultimate trophy proof
that you mean business

el chupacabras
la prueba definitiva de trofeos
que hablas en serio

elusive pipe dream
chasing *el chupacabras*
this is life so far

sueño elusivo y imposible
persiguiendo el chupacabras
así es la vida hasta ahora

new sport on the farm
"gone *chupacabra* tipping"
they never come back

nuevo deporte en la granja
"se fue a volcar el chupacabras"
nunca regresan

Chupacabra Flats:
where my broken heart lays
more space between us

Llano de Chupacabras:
donde yace mi corazón roto
más espacio entre nosotros

much rather listen
el chupacabras poet
deep in South Texas

prefiero escuchar
el poeta chupacabras
en lo profundo del sur de Tejas

only in Texas
does it rain armadillos
and… *chupacabras*

solo en Tejas
llueve armadillos
y… chupacabras

new hit TV show
"Married With *Chupacabras*"
getting high ratings

nuevo programa de televisión exitoso
"Casado Con Chupacabras"
obteniendo altas calificaciones

loves to write haiku
about wild *chupacabras*
chupacabristas

le encanta escribir haiku
sobre el chupacabras salvaje
chupacabristas

you know he is there
but the moon fools your own eyes
el chupacabras

sabes que el esta ahí
pero la luna engaña a tus propios ojos
el chupacabras

I don't always write
poems about *chupacabras*
…who am I kidding

no siempre escribo
poemas sobre chupacabras
…a quién estoy engañando

cry me a river
despair over the bodies
fat goats drained of life

puedes llorar todo lo que quieras
desesperación por los cuerpos
cabras gordas sin vida

peaceful chicken coop
where silence tears through morning
the last feather falls

gallinero pacífico
donde el silencio atraviesa la mañana
cae la última pluma

the circle of life
involving *chupacabras*
it's never pretty

el circulo de la vida
involucrando al chupacabras
nunca es bonito

turn away, don't look
for what it feeds upon now
may be your own pet

aléjate, no mires
por lo que se alimenta ahora
puede ser tu propia mascota

waiting in the woods
for those who say it's not real
el chupacabras

esperando en el bosque
para aquellos que dicen que no existe
el chupacabras

chupacabra smells
human pets and human fear
it's waiting for you

el chupacabras huele
mascotas y miedo humano
te esta esperando

fatal disaster
pretty blonde running through woods
falls… and drops poodle

desastre fatal
bonita rubia corriendo por el bosque
ella se cae… y su caniche también

goats, chickens, poodles
chupacabras do not care
for it is just food

cabras, gallinas, caniches
al chupacabras no le importa
porque es solo comida

can't you understand
to find *el chupacabras*
you must think like one

¿no puedes entender?
para encontrar al chupacabras
debes pensar como uno

running wild and free
chupcacabra code of life
there is no other

corriendo salvaje y libre
código de vida del chupacabras
no hay otro

once upon a time
something came crawling back home
eating all our dogs

érase una vez
algo vino arrastrándose de regreso a casa
comiendo a todos nuestros perros

crimes against chickens
not easy to overlook
bloody, feathered mess

crímenes contra gallinas
no es fácil pasarlo por alto
desastre sangriento y emplumado

sticking out of tents
supple hands are just as good
like a cornered hen

saliendo de las tiendas de campaña
las manos flexibles son igual de buenas
como una gallina acorralada

just outside your door
something gray calling on you
"let your pets come out"

justo afuera de tu puerta
algo gris llamándote
"deja salir a tus mascotas"

hidden in the night
something that should not exist
el chupacabras

escondido en la noche
algo que no debería existir
el chupacabras

handled correctly
a caged *chupacabras*
might not harm a soul

manejado correctamente
un chupacabras enjaulado
puede que no dañe un alma

endangered species
how the gray *chupacabras*
entered your mainstream

especie en peligro
como el chupacabras gris
entró en su corriente principal

horror is sitting
by the old dead mesquite tree
watching intently

el horror está sentado
junto al viejo mezquite muerto
mirando atentamente

what is a dinner
but a four-legged victim
free for consumption

que es una cena
pero una víctima de cuatro patas
gratis para el consumo

when writing freely
about *el chupacabras*
remember to growl

al escribir libremente
sobre el chupacabras
recuerda gruñir

imagination
the only proof between us
fear or not to fear

imaginación
la única prueba entre nosotros
temer o no temer

you believe in ghosts
I, in *el chupacabras*
which makes us less scared

tu crees en fantasmas
yo, en el chupacabras
cual nos hace temer menos

no matter what size
monster will be monster
chupacabra lives

no importa el tamaño
monstruo será monstruo
chupacabras viven

the dead grass crumbles
as the gray beast stalks its prey
under cool moon light

la hierba muerta se desmorona
mientras la bestia gris acecha a su presa
bajo la fresca luz de la luna

ever stop to think
if *el chupacabras* cares
whether it is real

alguna vez te detienes a pensar
si al chupacabras le importa
si es real

hard to concentrate
when hunger overtakes you
waiting days for chance

difícil de concentrar
cuando el hambre te alcanza
días esperando por la oportunidad

stillness of silence
unlike roar of a belly
loud into the dark night

quietud del silencio
a diferencia del rugido de un vientre
fuerte en la noche oscura

King *Chupacabras*
what they are calling me now
it suits me just fine

Rey Chupacabras
como me estan llamando ahora
me queda muy bien

hiding behind things
like we all expect you to
the humans from us

esconderse detrás de las cosas
como todos esperamos que lo hagas
los humanos de nosotros

wonder where it's been
check on your roosters and hens
dogs, cats and goats too

preguntan donde ha estado
revisa tus gallos y gallinas
perros, gatos y cabras también

el chupacabras
only looks out for itself
twisted loyalties

el chupacabras
solo mira por si mismo
lealtades retorcidas

the real truth is that
they exist, but they do not
play well with humans

la verdadera verdad es que
existen, pero no
juega bien con los humanos

chupacabra waits
for no one, nor a handout
it takes when it wants

chupacabras espera
para nadie, ni una limosna
se necesita cuando quiere

fresh, cool, morning dew
runs beautifully across
the goat's twisted face

fresco, rocío de la mañana
corre maravillosamente a través
la cara torcida de la cabra

envelope of dark
seals in your wildest fears
el chupacabras

sobre de oscuridad
sella tus miedos más salvajes
el chupacabras

it is very hard
to believe in your own eyes
goat-sucker is real

es muy difícil
creer en tus propios ojos
el chupacabras si existe

October is for
"Chupacabra Awareness"
not just Halloween

octubre es para
"Conciencia del Chupacabras"
no solo Halloween

throw them bleached bones
gamble with *chupacabras*
you already lost

arroja esos huesos secos
apuestas con el chupacabras
ya perdiste

there is no love lost
whether business or pleasure
for *chupacabras*

no hay amor perdido
ya sea negocios o placer
para chupacabras

why worry about
terrible *chupacabras*
worry about man

por qué te preocupas
con el terrible chupacabras
preocúpate con el hombre

trying hard to be
a good, gray *chupacabras*
goats still go missing

tratando duro de ser
un buen chupacabras gris
las cabras siguen desaparecidas

this forsaken place
serves roasted *chupacabras*
on platinum platters

este lugar abandonado
sirve chupacabras asado
en platos de platino

hungry and beastly
digging hard, a tunnel
under the pet shop

hambriento y bestial
cavando duro, un túnel
debajo de la tienda de mascotas

temple of the beast
where *chupacabra* secrets
remain unbroken

templo de la bestia
donde los secretos de chupacabras
permanecen intacto

knock down the front door
Pooh Bear inside his tree house
better than honey

rompe la puerta delantera
Oso Pooh dentro de su casa en el árbol
mejor que la miel

Goofy or Pluto
there is no difference in them
both dogs are good meals

Goofy o Plutón
no hay diferencia en ellos
ambos perros son buenas comidas

why did it turn out
me, the hunger; you, the meal
gray order of things

¿Por qué resultó?
yo, el hambre; tu, la comida
orden gris de las cosas

Jimmy Kimmel Show
with giant *chupacabras*
what in the world now

el show de Jimmy Kimmel
con chupacabras gigantes
¿Qué diablos pasa ahora?

yes, life is different
here among *chupacabras*
but why do you care

si, la vida es diferente
aquí entre chupacabras
pero ¿por qué te importa?

one thing is for sure
chupacabras don't ever
rat each other out

una cosa es segura
chupacabras nunca
delantan unos a otros

a *chupa-nado*:
when tornados pick up packs
of *chupacabras*

un chupa-nado:
cuando se levantan tornados
manadas de chupacabras

feel the fury of
the *Great Luchacabrador*
the wrestler of goats

siente la furia de
el Gran *Luchacabrador*
el luchador de cabras

many years from now
chupacabras will all laugh
target shots at you

dentro de muchos años
chupacabras se reirán
por tiros dirigidos a ti

forget the bad wolf
there's something worse in the woods
my red, riding hood

olvidate del lobo malo
hay algo peor en el bosque
mi caperucita roja

Chupacabra Chicks:
nice looking humans selling
chupacabra shirts

Chicas Chupacabras:
hembras guapas vendiendo
camisas de chupacabras

like goats in the night
taken out one at a time
somebody's hungry

como cabras en la noche
sacado uno a la vez
alguien tiene hambre

then I saw "its" face
now I'm a believer
no doubt in my mind

entonces vi "su" cara
ahora soy un creyente
no hay duda en mi mente

Hey, we're the Chupas
and we like to chupa around!
…quickly, hide your goats

Oye, somos los Chupas
¡Y nos gusta chupar!
…rápido, esconde tus cabras

once upon a goat
whose life ended at the throat
so says those that gloat

érase una cabra
cuya vida terminó en la garganta
eso dicen los que se regodean

it was strange indeed
dreaming of *chupacabras*
never be the same

fue realmente extraño
soñar con chupacabras
nunca seré el mismo

About the Author

Juan Manuel Pérez, a Mexican-American poet of Indigenous descent and the Poet Laureate for Corpus Christi, Texas (2019-2020), is the author of numerous poetry books including the award-wining, poetic-memoir, THIRTY YEARS AGO: LIFE AND THE FIRST GULF WAR (2023) and the Mexican-American Barrio Horror Novel-In-Verse, LA SANTA MADRE TAMALERA (2023). Juan, is also the 2021 Horror Authors Guild's Inaugural Lifetime Achievement Award winner and a recipient of a 2021 Horror Writers Association Diversity Grant. This poet's credits also include one recent Honorable Mention in the 2025 Inaugural War Poetry Postcard Contest, a 2024 Regal Summit Book Award, two Aphelion's Best Poetry Of The Year Listings (2023, 2024), two Pushcart Prize Nominations (2017, 2023), three Elgin Book Award Nominations (2021, 2022, 2023), four Rhysling Award Nominations (2011, 2012, 2013, 2020), four Dwarf Star Award Nominations (2012, 2020, 2021, 2022) with one Honorable Mention win in 2022, and one H.E.R.O.I.C. People's Choice Award Nomination (2024).

Juan's maternal lineage flows through the Purépecha and Otomi people. Currently, the family is also verifying their alleged descendancy to Emperor Moctezuma Xocoyotzin II through this same line after Ancestry DNA family tree links led to said conclusion. Additionally, relational ties to the mythological Quinametzin, the Indigenous giants of Mexico who purportedly built some of the older pyramids of Mexico, have traditionally been a part of the family's stories. His paternal lineage runs through the Coahuiltecanos, or Indigenous Tejanos, and the modern day Xicanos.

In the mid-1990's while still in the military, he was inducted into the Memphis Tia-Piah Big River Clan Warrior Society, a Gourd Dancer Society, and has served on several pow-wow committees and associations as a board member and organizer, as well as leading Red Thunder, a color guard made up of Indigenous Veterans and active-duty service members. While a part of these Tennessee Indigenous associations, Juan and his wife, Dr. Malia Ann Perez, and their two children, along with other various peoples associated with the Mississippi Delta, were part of the historic Great Chickasaw Nation's First Annual Homecoming Celebration on November 5, 1994. This event was literally the "Restaging of The Trail Of Tears" which included a ferry/barge crossing (sponsored by the US Army Corps of Engineers) from the Arkansas side onto Mud Island on the Memphis, Tennessee side. Then, after remarks from city officials, they traveled to Desoto Park on the Fourth Chickasaw Bluff which was to be renamed "Chickasaw Heritage Park." This "Rendezvous On The River" as it was promoted was also symbolically called the "Reverse Trail Of Tears."

Juan is also a Marine-Regulation Navy Corpsman, a Fleet Marine Force "Doc," that served between 1987 and 1997 who was deployed to Desert Shield/Desert Storm in 1990-1991 with the 2nd Marines ground forces and was also part of the Special Marine Air Ground Task Force deployed to assist devastated Homestead, Florida for the Hurricane Andrew Relief in 1992. In that deployment, Juan was one of the specialized field medics and Spanish language translators for the 2nd Medical Battalion, 2nd

Force Service Support Group out of Camp Lejeune, North Carolina.

Juan currently Gourd Dances around the Lone Star State with a loose confederacy of Indigenous warriors from Central and South Texas, and also works as a Certified Public High School History Teacher and promotes poetry, as well as, Indigenous / Mexican / Mexican-American History when and where he can.

To learn more about this award-winning poet, migrant field worker, combat vet, history teacher, and Native American Gourd Dancer, please check out his official website at: https://www.juanmperez.com/

www.ingramcontent.com/pod-product-compliance
Lightning Source LLC
Chambersburg PA
CBHW010936120626
46554CB00007B/2496